his book belongs to:

Table of Co

CW00505854

All of the wonderful
and beautifully made women
of our most high God, Jesus Christ.

This book is part of
a Holy Spirit filled series
just for us women.

Daily scriptures that will help us cope every day
and take us into Jesus arms to protect our hearts,
emotions, spirits and minds in this world of uncertainty.

To help us with our homes, marriages, children
and guide us to make the best decisions in our daily walk.

Also to know what our roles are
as Godly women
and what is expected from us
to enter the Kingdom of our God one day.

Prophecy is not merely to foretell
or to write inspirited Scriptures,
but for edification, exhortation and comfort,
and will be done away (1 Cor. 13:8) at such time
as the Church no longer needs edification
but is made perfect in love (1 Cor. 13:10),
which is far from the case at this time.

Lastly shows that when the daughters prophesied
out of there spirits, the words of there mouth
will utter the Holy Spirit.

Let us all love and show love like Jesus.
That our lives will reflect
the most wonderful light of God.
Shinning brighter than the biggest, highest
and heavenly radiant star.

Heaps of hugs and blessings Lovely Lady's.

Annalien Lenk

Woman's
Worship
mighty
anointed
named
Savior

Bible Verses about Woman

Book
before
opening
pouring
knowing

Daily Prayer

-2

Dear Lord my God, I pray for the person
reading this prayer today.
I pray for strength, faith and courage.
Strength to go through any tough situation.

Faith as big as the highest mountain and the deepest sea.

Courage to solve and sought thru the highest situations in life.

I pray for any hurt, unhappiness, healing and all situations
that are out of their hands to be solved and finished
through the power of the blood of Jesus.

Let the world be driven by God's love and peace today
as they step up and out.

May their day be filled with goodness and mercy.

This I pray in the all mighty name of Jesus, son of God.

Amen

Prayer by Annalien Lenk

Favour is deceitful, and beauty is vain:

but a woman that feareth the Lord, she shall be praised.

Proverbs 31:30 King James Version

God is in the midst of her;

she shall not be moved:

God shall help her,
and that right early.

Psalm 46:5 kjv

The aged women likewise,
that they be in behaviour
as becometh holiness,
not false accusers,
not given to much wine,
teachers of good things;

That they may teach the young women
to be sober, to love their husbands,
to love their children,

To be discreet, chaste,
keepers at home, good,
obedient to their own husbands,
that the word of God
be not blasphemed.

Titus 2:3-5 kjv

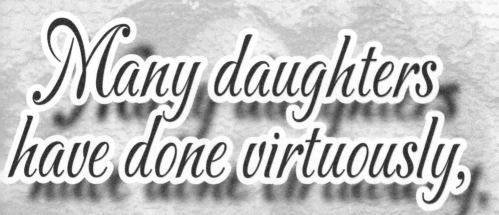

Many daughters have done virtuously,

but thou excellest them all.

Proverbs 31:29 kjv

Wives, submit yourselves
unto your own husbands,
as unto the Lord.

For the husband
is the head of the wife, even
as Christ is the head of the church:

and he is the saviour
of the body.

Therefore as the church
is subject unto Christ,
so let the wives be
to their own husbands
in every thing.

Ephesians 5:22-24 kjv

*Strength
and honour
are her clothing;*

*and she shall rejoice
in time to come.*

Proverbs 31:25 kjv

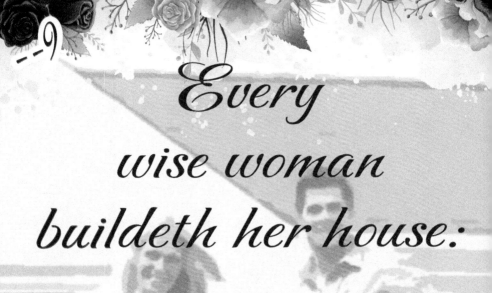

Every wise woman buildeth her house:

but the foolish plucketh it down with her hands

Proverbs 14:1 kjv

I will praise thee;
for I am fearfully
and wonderfully made:

marvellous are thy works;

and that my soul
knoweth right well.

Psalm 139:14 kjv

Let the woman learn
in silence with all subjection.

But I suffer not a woman
to teach, nor to usurp authority
over the man, but to be in silence.

For Adam
was first formed,
then Eve.

And Adam was not deceived,
but the woman being deceived
was in the transgression.

Notwithstanding
she shall be saved in childbearing,
if they continue in faith and charity
and holiness with sobriety.

1 Timothy 2:11-15 kjv

She considereth
a field, and buyeth it:

with the fruit of her hands
she planteth a vineyard.

She girdeth her loins with strength,
and strengtheneth her arms.

Proverbs 31:16-17 kjv

-13

Thou shalt also be a crown of glory in the hand of the Lord, and a royal diadem in the hand of thy God.

Isaiah 62:3 kjv

Even so must their wives be grave, not slanderers, sober, faithful in all things.

1 Timothy 3: 11 kjv

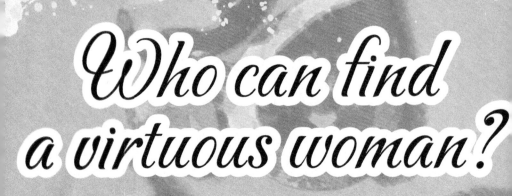

Who can find a virtuous woman?

for her price is far above rubies.

Proverbs 31:10 kjv

-16

The Lord
is my strength
and my shield;

my heart trusted in him,
and I am helped:

therefore
my heart greatly rejoiceth;

and with my song
will I praise him.

Psalm 28:7 kjv

-17

For God
is not the author of confusion,
but of peace,
as in all churches of the saints.

Let your women
keep silence in the churches:

for it is not permitted
unto them to speak;

but they are
commanded to be under obedience
as also saith the law.

And if they will learn any thing,
let them ask their husbands at hom

for it is a shame for women
to speak in the church.

1   Corinthians 14:33 -35 kjv

*And blessed is she
that believed:*

*for there shall be a performance
of those things
which were told her
from the Lord.*

Luke 1:45 kjv

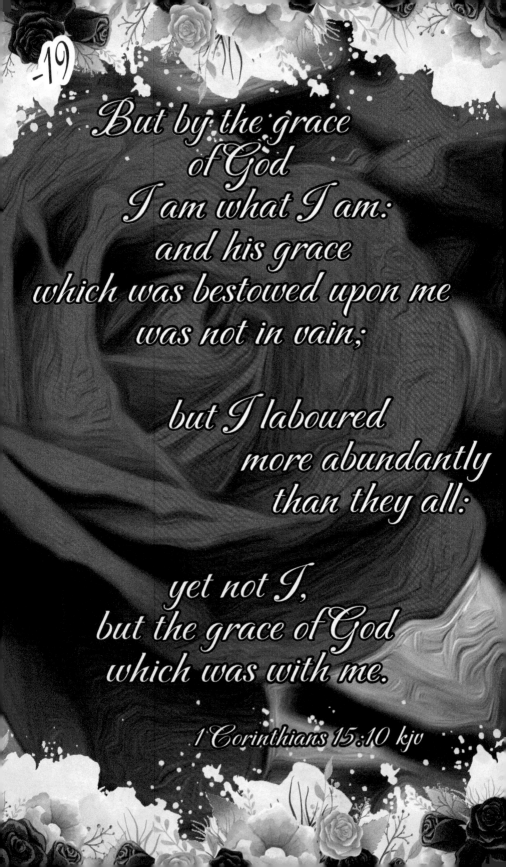

-19

But by the grace
of God
I am what I am:
and his grace
which was bestowed upon me
was not in vain;

but I laboured
more abundantly
than they all:

yet not I,
but the grace of God
which was with me.

1 Corinthians 15:10 kjv

A gracious woman
retaineth honour:

and strong men
retain riches.

Proverbs 11:16 kjv

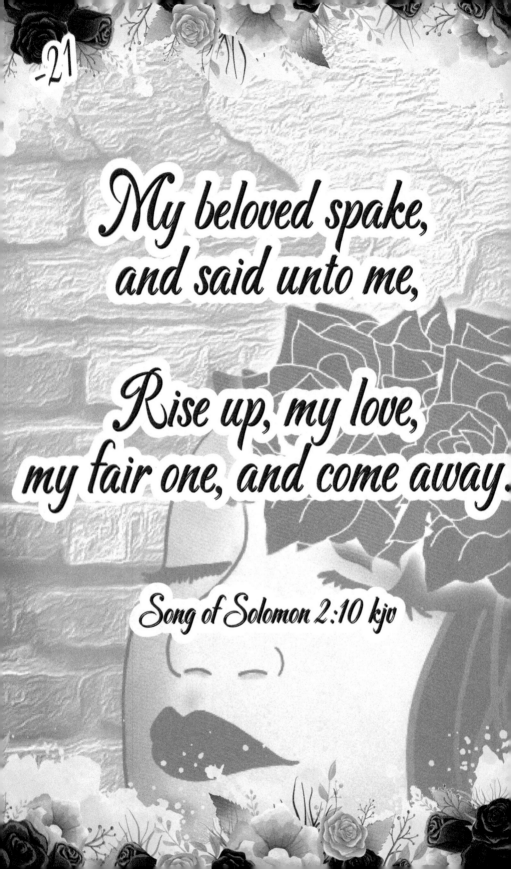

My beloved spake,
and said unto me,

Rise up, my love,
my fair one, and come away.

Song of Solomon 2:10 kjv

For as the woman
is of the man,
even so is the man
also by the woman;

but all things of God.

1 Corinthians 11:12 kjv

-23

1 Corinthians 11:3-16 kjv

But I would have you know,
that the head of every man is Christ;
and the head of the woman is the man,
and the head of Christ is God.

Every man praying or prophesying,
having his head covered,
dishonoureth his head.

But every woman
that prayeth or prophesieth
with her head uncovered
dishonoureth her head:
for that is even all one
as if she were shaven.

For if the woman be not covered,
let her also be shorn:
but if it be a shame for a woman
to be shorn or shaven, let her be covered.

For a man indeed
ought not to cover his head,
forasmuch as he is the image
and glory of God:

but the woman is the glory of the man.

For the man is not of the woman:
but the woman of the man.

Neither was the man created
for the woman;
but the woman for the man.

For this cause ought the woman
to have power on...

She girdeth her loins with strength, and strengtheneth her arms.

Proverbs 31:17 kjv

26

She stretcheth out her hand
to the poor;

yea, she reacheth forth her hands
to the needy.

She is not afraid
of the snow for her household:
for all her household
are clothed with scarlet.

Proverbs 31:20-21 kjv

-28

She openeth
her mouth with wisdom;

and in her tongue
is the law of kindness.

Proverbs 31:26 kjv

-29

Be careful for nothing;
but in every thing by prayer
and supplication
with thanksgiving let your requests
be made known unto God.

And the peace of God,
which passeth all understanding,
shall keep your hearts
and minds through Christ Jesus.

Philippians 4:6-7 kjv

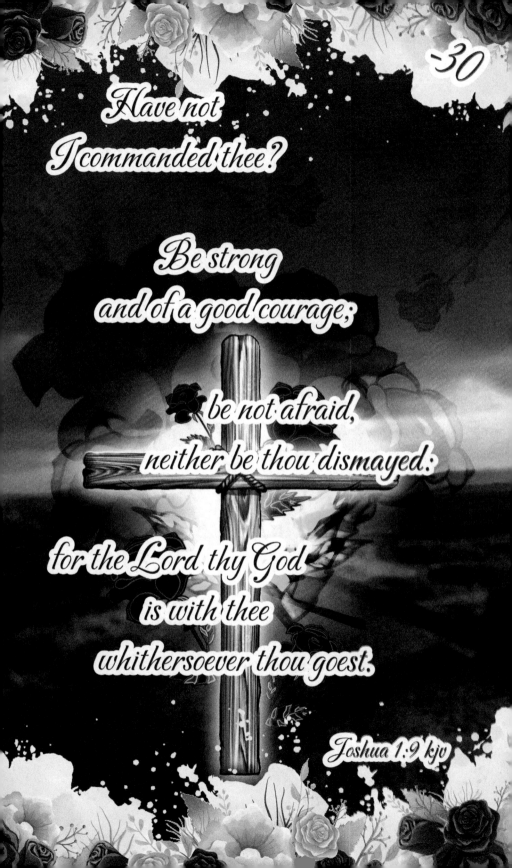

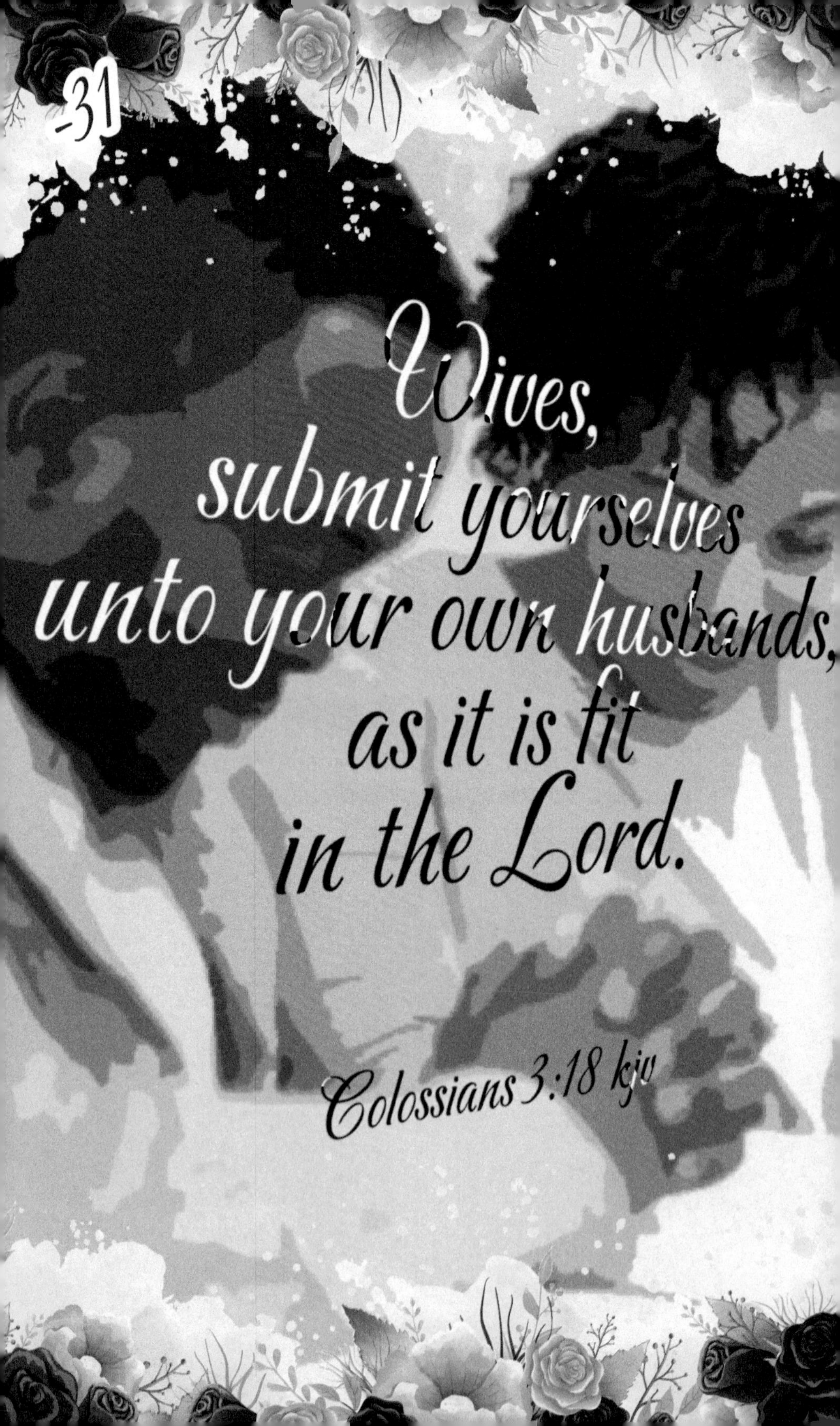

31

Wives,
submit yourselves
unto your own husbands,
as it is fit
in the Lord.

Colossians 3:18 kjv

They looked unto him, and were lightened:

and their faces were not ashamed.

Psalm 34:5 kjv

Her children arise up,
and call her blessed;

her husband also,
and he praiseth her.

Proverbs 31:28 kjv

My flesh
and my heart faileth:

but God
is the strength of my heart,
and my portion for ever.

Psalm 73:26·kjv

For thou hast possessed

my reins:

thou hast covered me

in my mother's womb

I will praise thee;

for I am fearfully

and wonderfully made:

marvellous are thy works;

and that my soul

knoweth right well.

Psalm 139:13-14 kjv

I will praise thee,
O Lord,
with my whole heart;

I will shew forth
all thy marvellous works.

Psalm 9:1 kjv

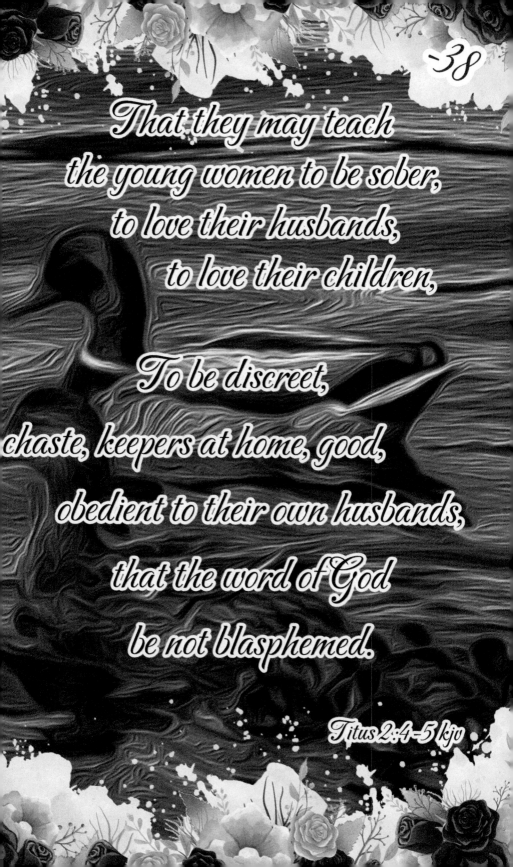

That they may teach
the young women to be sober,
to love their husbands,
to love their children,

To be discreet,
chaste, keepers at home, good,
obedient to their own husbands,
that the word of God
be not blasphemed.

Titus 2:4-5 kjv

39

For we are his workmanship, created in Christ Jesus unto good works, which God hath before ordained that we should walk in them.

Ephesians 2:10 kjv

Finally, brethren,

whatsoever things are true,

whatsoever things are honest,

whatsoever things are just,

whatsoever things are pure,

whatsoever things are lovely,

whatsoever things are of good report;

if there be any virtue,

and if there be any praise,

think on these things.

Philippians 4:8 kjv

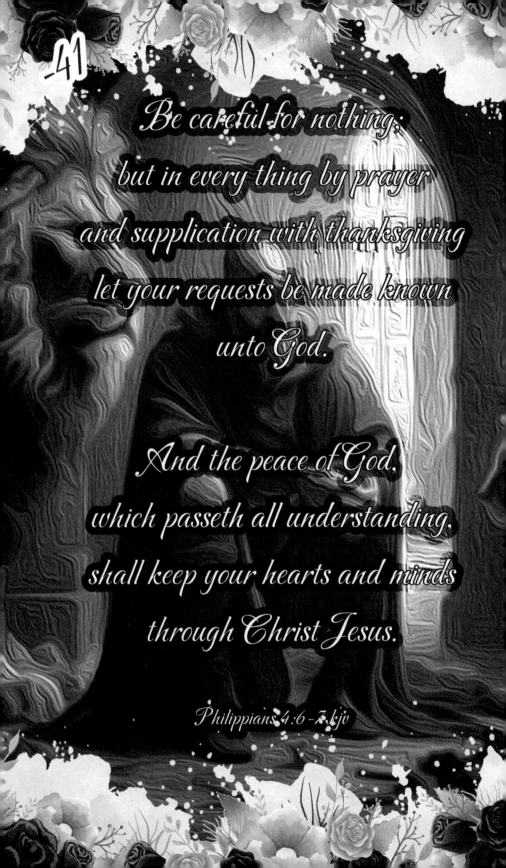

Be careful for nothing;
but in every thing by prayer
and supplication with thanksgiving
let your requests be made known
unto God.

And the peace of God,
which passeth all understanding,
shall keep your hearts and minds
through Christ Jesus.

Philippians 4:6-7 kjv

Likewise, ye wives, be in subjection
to your own husbands;
that, if any obey not the word,
they also may without the word
be won by the conversation of the wives;

While they behold your chaste conversation
coupled with fear.
Whose adorning let it not be that outward adorning
of plaiting the hair, and of wearing of gold,
or of putting on of apparel;

But let it be the hidden man of the heart,
in that which is not corruptible,
even the ornament of a meek and quiet spirit,
which is in the sight of God of great price.
For after this manner in the old time
the holy women also,
who trusted in God, adorned themselves,
being in subjection unto their own husbands:

Even as Sara obeyed Abraham, calling him lord:
whose daughters ye are, as long as ye do well,
and are not afraid with any amazement.

1 Peter 3:1-6 kjv

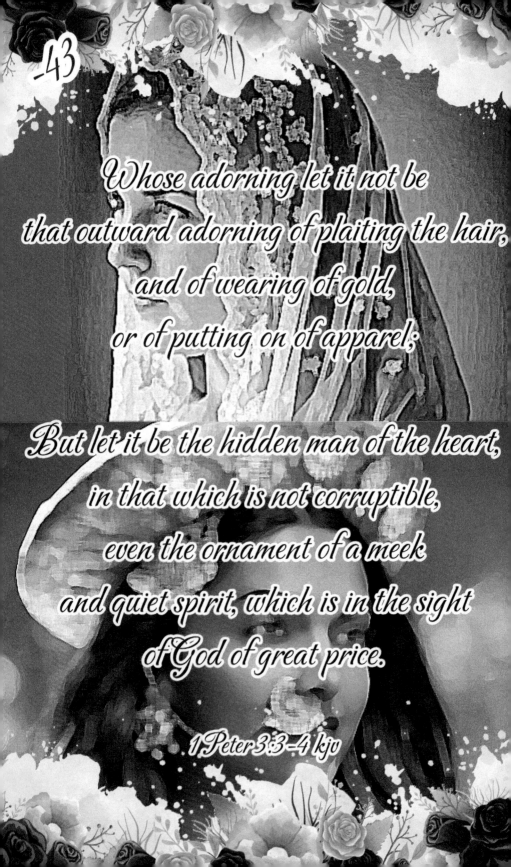

43

Whose adorning let it not be
that outward adorning of plaiting the hair,
and of wearing of gold,
or of putting on of apparel;

But let it be the hidden man of the heart,
in that which is not corruptible,
even the ornament of a meek
and quiet spirit, which is in the sight
of God of great price.

1 Peter 3:3-4 kjv

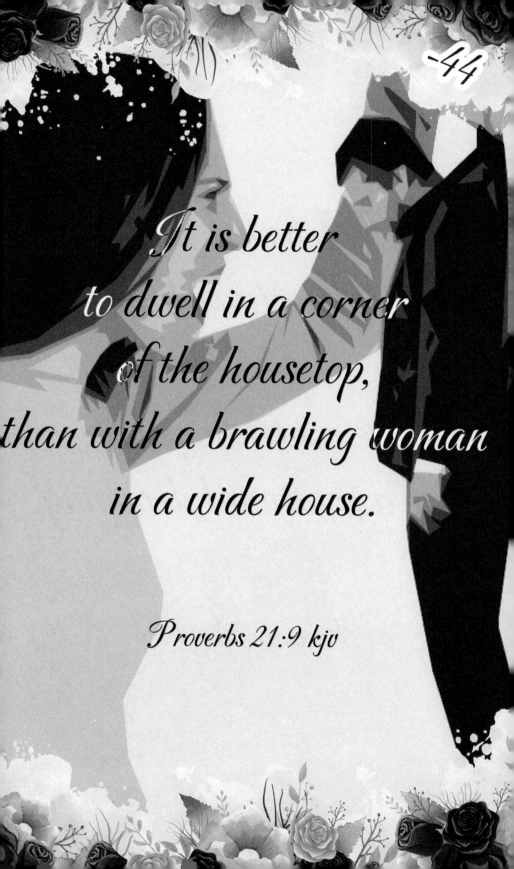

It is better
to dwell in a corner
of the housetop,
than with a brawling woman
in a wide house.

Proverbs 21:9 kjv

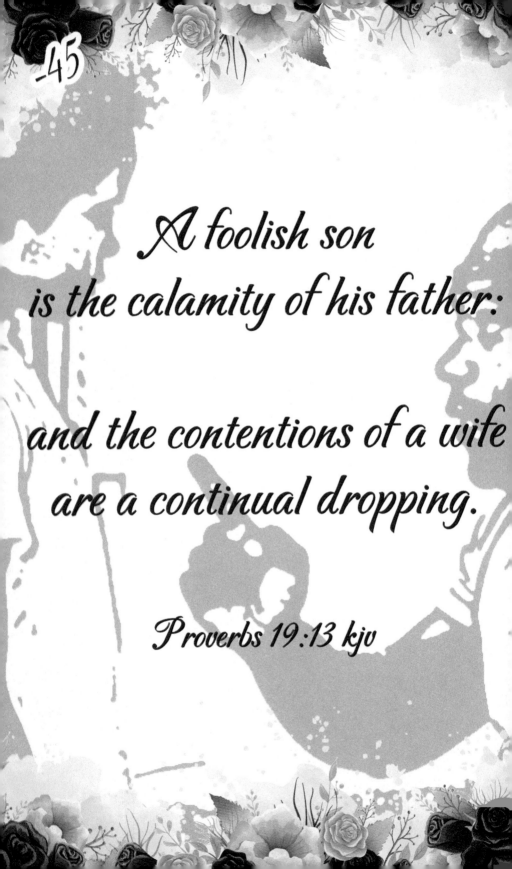

*A foolish son
is the calamity of his father:*

*and the contentions of a wife
are a continual dropping.*

Proverbs 19:13 kjv

She is more precious
than rubies:

and all the things
thou canst desire
are not to be compared
unto her.

Proverbs 3:15 kjv

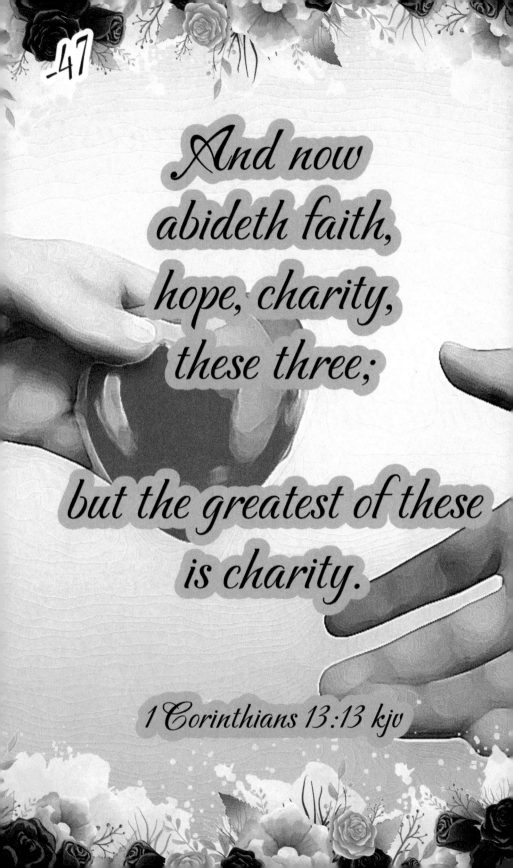

And now abideth faith, hope, charity, these three; but the greatest of these is charity.

1 Corinthians 13:13 kjv

Trust in the Lord
with all thine heart;
and lean not
unto thine own understanding.

In all thy ways
acknowledge him,
and he shall direct
thy paths.

Proverbs 3:5-6 kjv

Colossians 3:12-21 kjv

Put on therefore, as the elect of God,

holy and beloved, bowels of mercies,

kindness, humbleness of mind,

meekness, longsuffering;

Forbearing one another,
and forgiving one another,
if any man have a quarrel
against any:

even as Christ forgave you,
so also do ye.

And above all these things
put on charity,
which is the bond of perfectness.

And let the peace of God
rule in your hearts,
to the which also ye are called in one body;

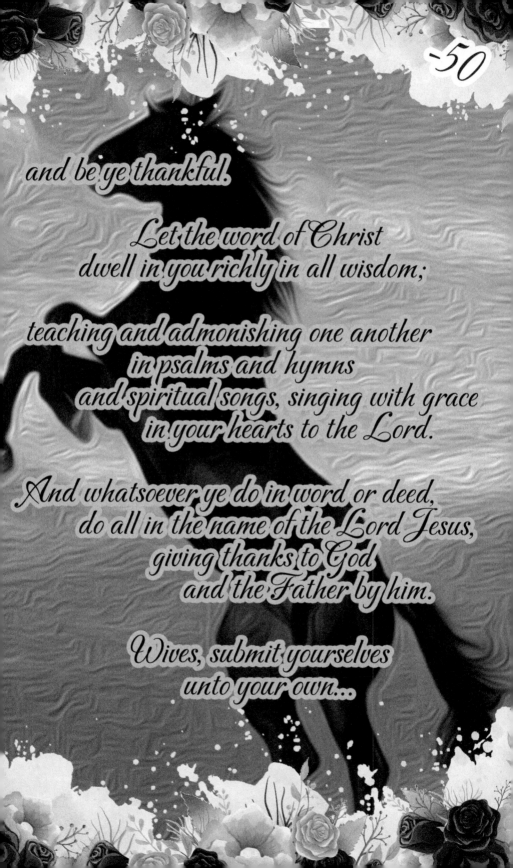

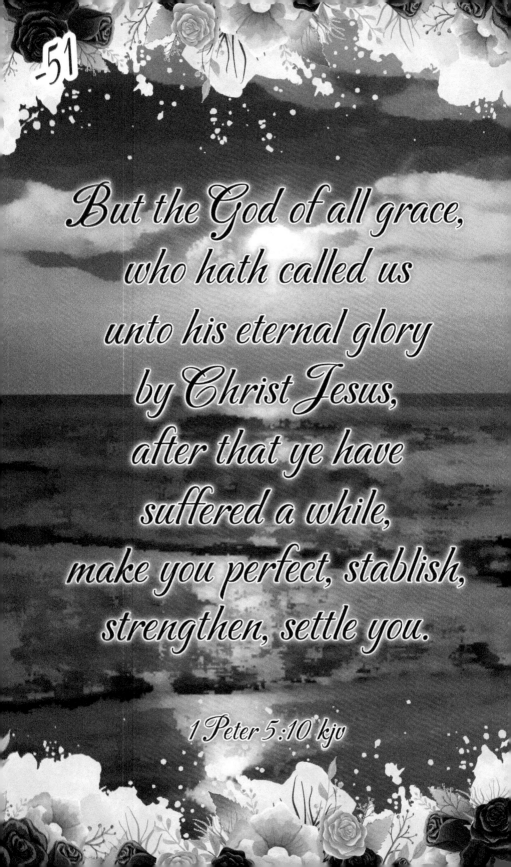

-51

But the God of all grace,
who hath called us
unto his eternal glory
by Christ Jesus,
after that ye have
suffered a while,
make you perfect, stablish,
strengthen, settle you.

1 Peter 5:10 kjv

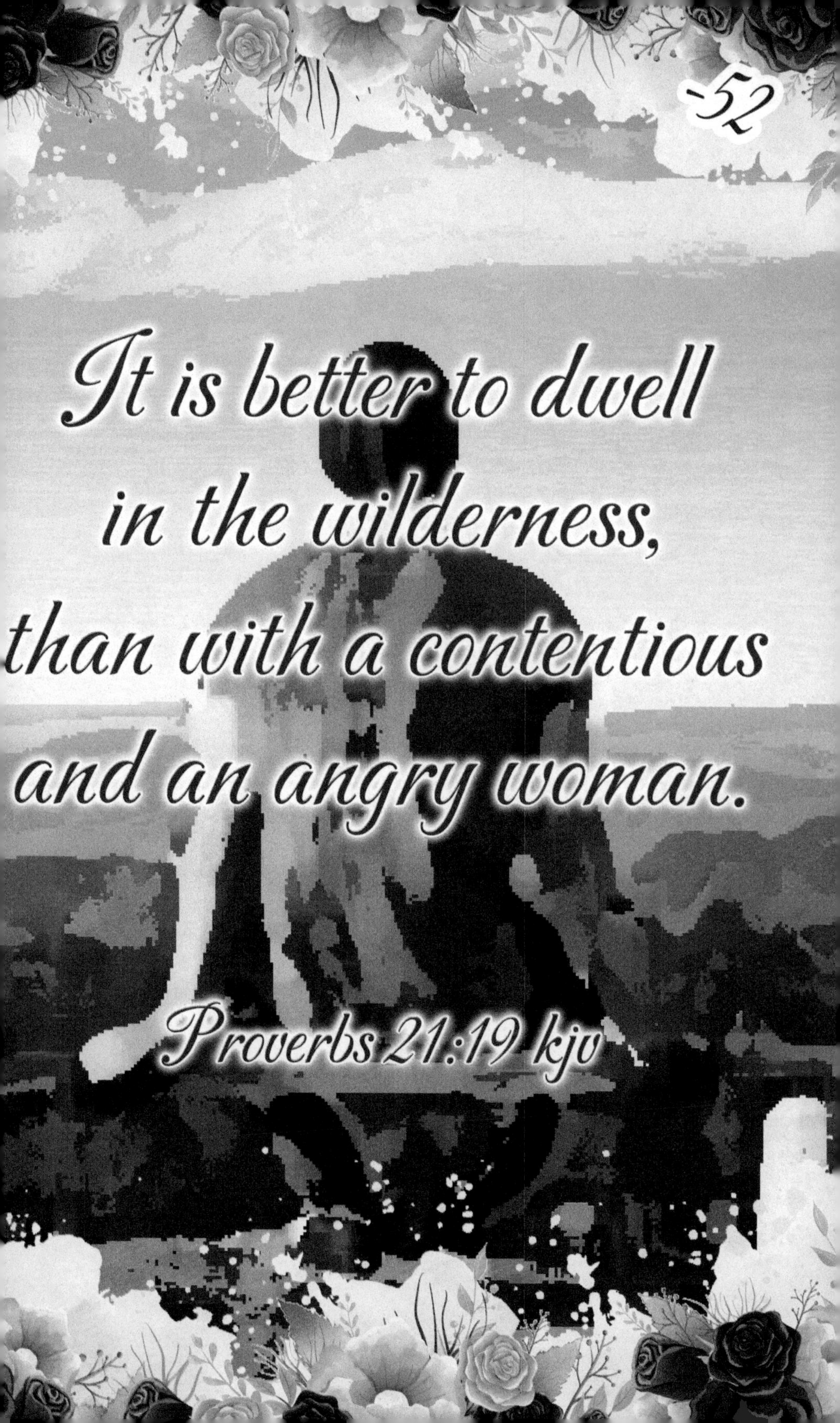

It is better to dwell
in the wilderness,
than with a contentious
and an angry woman.

Proverbs 21:19 kjv

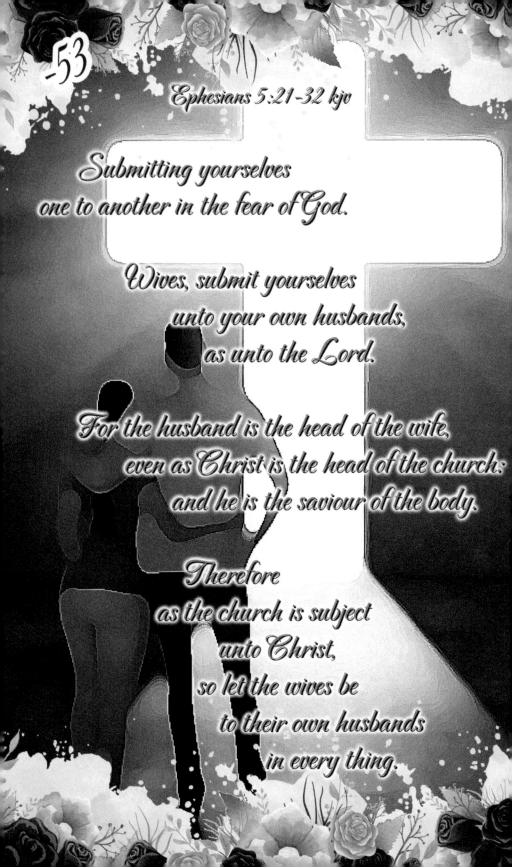

Ephesians 5:21-32 kjv

Submitting yourselves
one to another in the fear of God.

Wives, submit yourselves
unto your own husbands,
as unto the Lord.

For the husband is the head of the wife,
even as Christ is the head of the church:
and he is the saviour of the body.

Therefore
as the church is subject
unto Christ,
so let the wives be
to their own husbands
in every thing.

-54

Husbands, love your wives,
even as Christ also loved the church,
and gave himself for it;

That he might sanctify
and cleanse it with the washing of water
by the word,

That he might present it to himself
a glorious church,
not having spot, or wrinkle,
or any such thing;

but that it should be holy
and without blemish.

So ought men to love their wives as
their own bodies.

He that loveth his wife
loveth himself.

For no man
ever yet hated his own.

Proverbs 31:10 -31 kjv

Who can find a virtuous woman?

for her price is far above rubies.

The heart of her husband

doth safely trust in her,

so that he shall have no need of spoil.

She will do him good

and not evil all the days of her life.

She seeketh wool, and flax,

and worketh willingly with her hands.

She is like the merchants' ships;

she bringeth her food from afar.

She riseth also while it is yet night,

and giveth meat to her household,

and a portion to her maidens.

She considereth a field, and buyeth it:
with the fruit of her hands
she planteth a vineyard.

She girdeth her loins with strength,
and strengtheneth her arms.

She perceiveth that her merchandise is good:
her candle goeth not out by night.

She layeth her hands to the spindle,
and her hands hold the distaff.

*Likewise,
ye wives, be in subjection
to your own husbands;
that, if any obey not the word,
they also may
without the word
be won by the conversation
of the wives;*

*While they behold
your chaste conversation
coupled with fear.*

1 Peter 3:1-2 kjv

-58

For I know the thoughts
that I think toward you,
saith the Lord,

thoughts of peace,
and not of evil,
to give you an
expected end.

Jeremiah 29:11 kjv

But ye
are a chosen generation,
a royal priesthood,
an holy nation,
a peculiar people;
that ye should shew forth
the praises of him
who hath called you
out of darkness
into his marvellous light;

1 Peter 2:9 kjv

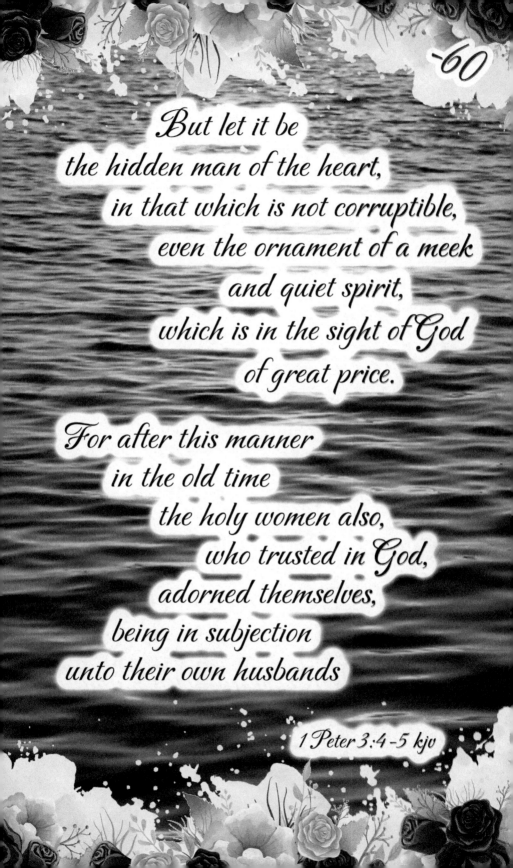

But let it be
the hidden man of the heart,
in that which is not corruptible,
even the ornament of a meek
and quiet spirit,
which is in the sight of God
of great price.

For after this manner
in the old time
the holy women also,
who trusted in God,
adorned themselves,
being in subjection
unto their own husbands

1 Peter 3:4–5 kjv

-61

1 Corinthians 13:4-8 kjv

Charity suffereth long,
and is kind;
charity envieth not;
charity vaunteth not itself,
is not puffed up,

Doth not behave itself unseemly,
seeketh not her own,
is not easily provoked,
thinketh no evil;

Rejoiceth not in iniquity,
but rejoiceth in the truth;

Beareth all things,
believeth all things,
hopeth all things,
endureth all things.

Charity never faileth:
but whether there be prophecies,
they shall fail;
whether there be tongues,
they shall cease;
whether there be knowledge,
it shall vanish away.

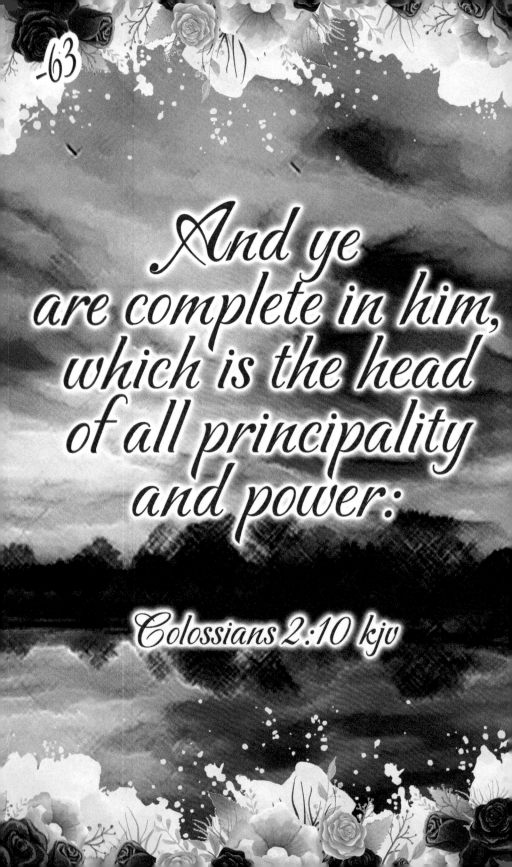

And ye
are complete in him,
which is the head
of all principality
and power:

Colossians 2:10 kjv

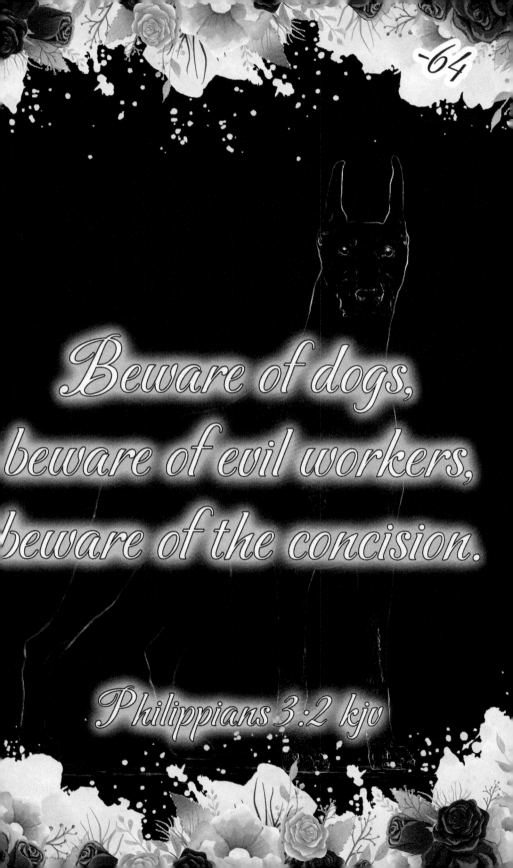

Beware of dogs, beware of evil workers, beware of the concision.

Philippians 3:2 kjv

-65

But they
that wait upon the Lord
shall renew their strength,

they shall mount up
with wings as eagles;

they shall run,
and not be weary;
and they shall walk,
and not faint.

Isaiah 40:31 kjv

For God
hath not given us
the spirit of fear;

but of power,
and of love,
and of a sound mind.

2 Timothy 1:7 kjv

But the Lord said
unto Samuel,
Look not on his countenance,
or on the height
of his stature;

because I have refused him:
for the Lord
seeth not as man seeth;
for man looketh
on the outward appearance,
but the Lord looketh
on the heart.

1 Samuel 16:7 kjv

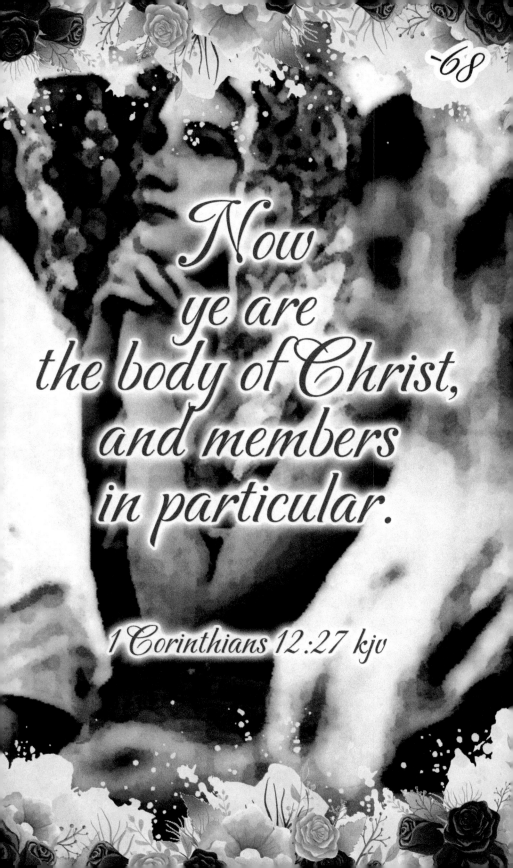

Now
ye are
the body of Christ,
and members
in particular.

1 Corinthians 12:27 kjv

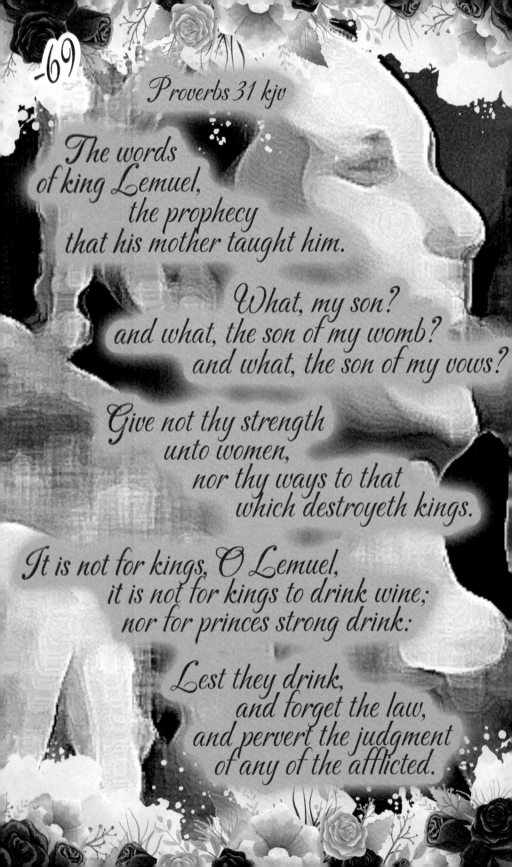

69

Proverbs 31 kjv

The words
of king Lemuel,
      the prophecy
that his mother taught him.

What, my son?
and what, the son of my womb?
      and what, the son of my vows?

Give not thy strength
      unto women,
            nor thy ways to that
                  which destroyeth kings.

It is not for kings, O Lemuel,
      it is not for kings to drink wine;
            nor for princes strong drink:

Lest they drink,
      and forget the law,
      and pervert the judgment
            of any of the afflicted.

Give strong drink unto him
that is ready to perish,
and wine unto those
that be of heavy hearts.

Let him drink,
and forget his poverty,
and remember his misery no more.

Open thy mouth for
the dumb in the cause of all
such as are appointed
to destruction.

Open thy mouth,
judge righteously,
and plead the cause
of the poor and needy.

Who can find a virtuous woman?
for her price is far above...

Genesis 2:18–24 kjv

And the Lord God said,
It is not good
that the man should be alone;

I will make him an help
meet for him.

And out of the ground
the Lord God formed
every beast of the field,
and every fowl of the air;

and brought them unto Adam
to see what he would call them:

and whatsoever
Adam called every living creature,
that was the name thereof.

And Adam
gave names to all cattle,
and to the fowl of the air,
and to every beast of the field;

but for Adam
there was not found an help
meet for him.

And the Lord God
caused a deep sleep
to fall upon Adam,
and he slept:

and he took one of his ribs,
and closed up the flesh
instead thereof;

And the rib,
which the Lord God had taken
from man,
made he a woman,
and brought her unto the man.

And Adam said,
This is now bone of my bones,
and flesh of my flesh:...

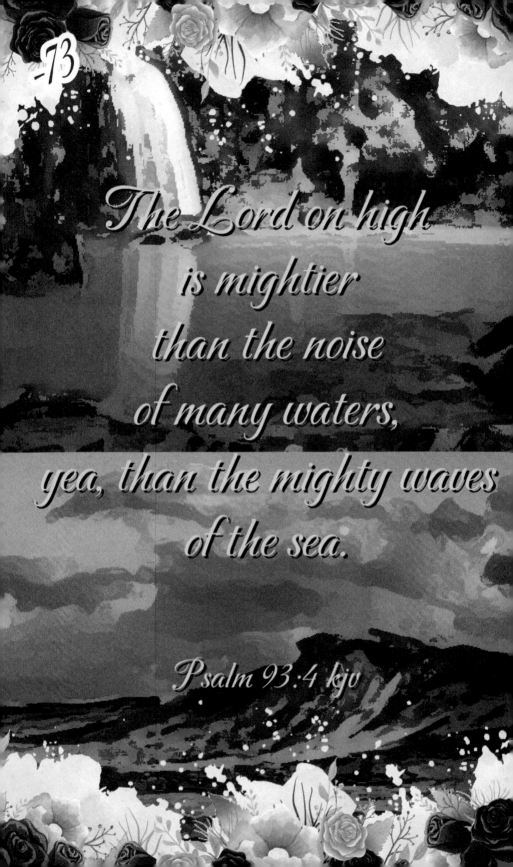

The Lord on high
is mightier
than the noise
of many waters,
yea, than the mighty waves
of the sea.

Psalm 93:4 kjv

*He shall not
be afraid of
evil tidings:*

*his heart is fixed,
trusting
in the Lord.*

Psalm 112:7 kjv

The Lord
shall fight for you,
and ye
shall hold your peace.

Exodus 14:14 kjv

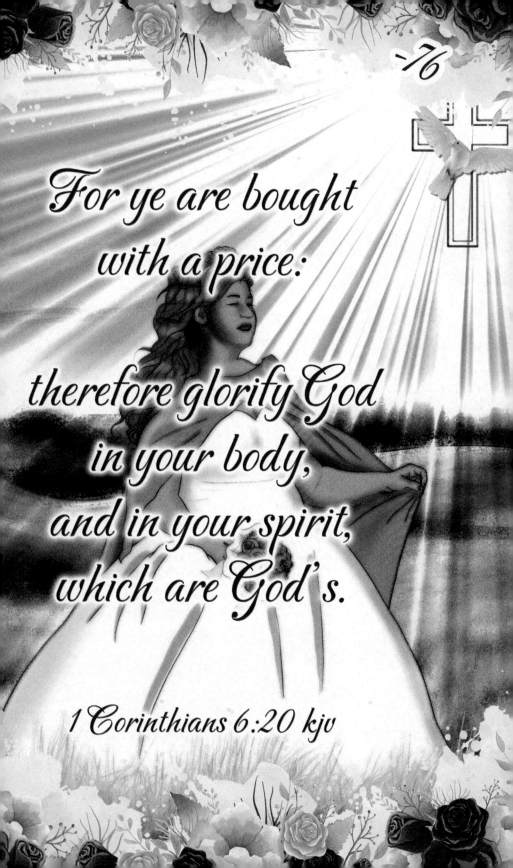

For ye are bought
with a price:

therefore glorify God
in your body,
and in your spirit,
which are God's.

1 Corinthians 6:20 kjv

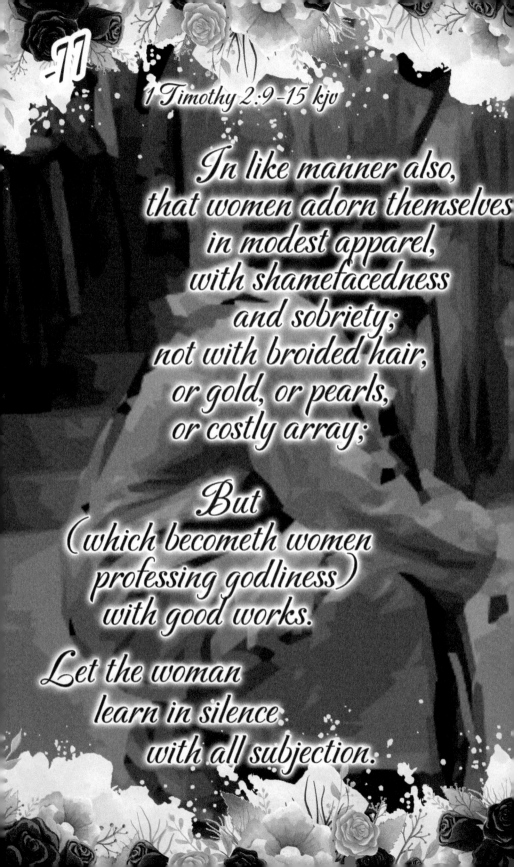

1 Timothy 2:9-15 kjv

In like manner also,
that women adorn themselves
in modest apparel,
with shamefacedness
and sobriety;
not with broided hair,
or gold, or pearls,
or costly array;

But
(which becometh women
professing godliness)
with good works.

Let the woman
learn in silence
with all subjection.

But I suffer not
a woman to teach,
nor to usurp authority
over the man,
but to be in silence.

For Adam
was first formed,
then Eve.

And Adam was not deceived,
but the woman being deceived
was in the transgression.

Notwithstanding
she shall be saved
in childbearing,
if they continue in faith
and charity
and holiness
with sobriety.

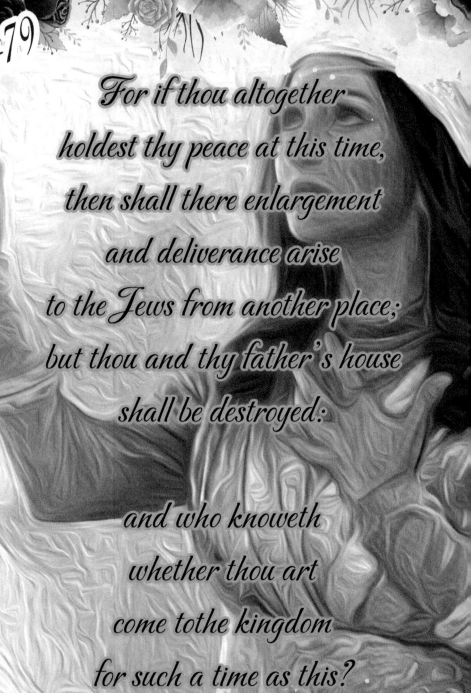

For if thou altogether
holdest thy peace at this time,
then shall there enlargement
and deliverance arise
to the Jews from another place;
but thou and thy father's house

shall be destroyed:

and who knoweth
whether thou art
come tothe kingdom
for such a time as this?

Esther 4:14 kjv

-80

Honour thy
father and mother;
which is
the first commandment
with promise;

That it may be
well with thee,
and thou mayest
live long
on the earth.

Ephesians 6:2-3 kjv

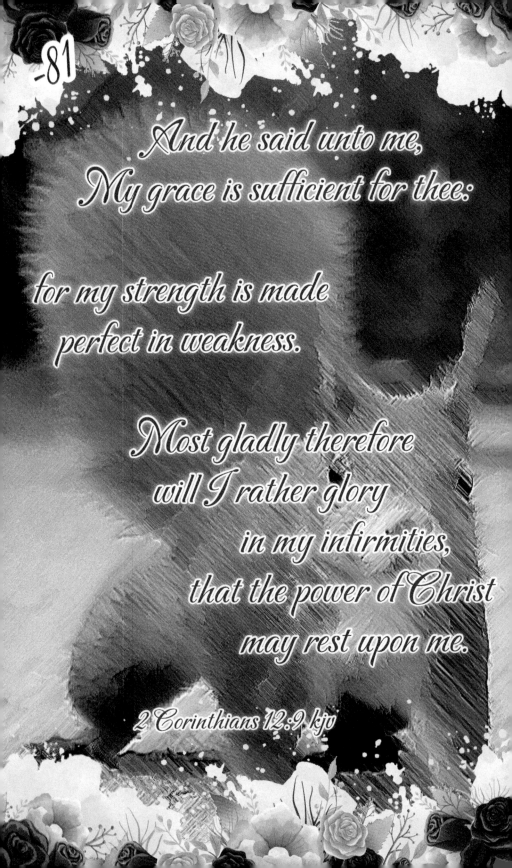

-81

And he said unto me,
My grace is sufficient for thee:

for my strength is made
perfect in weakness.

Most gladly therefore
will I rather glory
in my infirmities,
that the power of Christ
may rest upon me.

2 Corinthians 12:9 kjv

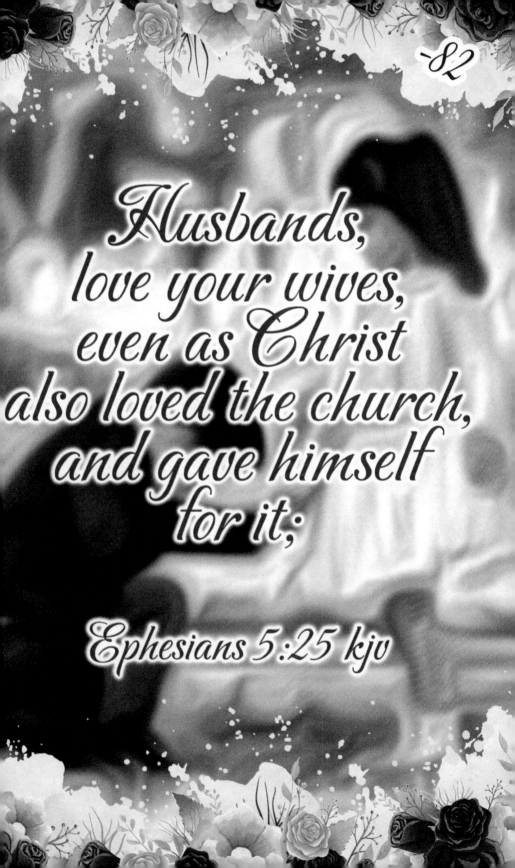

Husbands,
love your wives,
even as Christ
also loved the church,
and gave himself
for it;

Ephesians 5:25 kjv

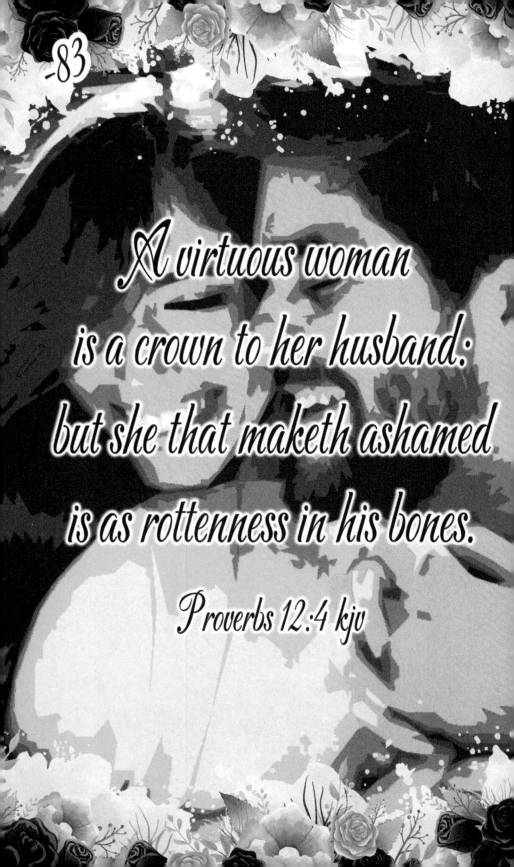

A virtuous woman
is a crown to her husband:
but she that maketh ashamed
is as rottenness in his bones.

Proverbs 12:4 kjv

Behold,

I have graven thee

upon the palms of my hands;

thy walls

are continually before me.

Isaiah 49:16 kjv

They are new

every morning:

great is
thy faithfulness.

Lamentations 3:23 kjv

Ye are of God,
little children,
and have overcome them:

because greater is he
that is in you,
than he
that is in the world.

1 John 4:4 kjv

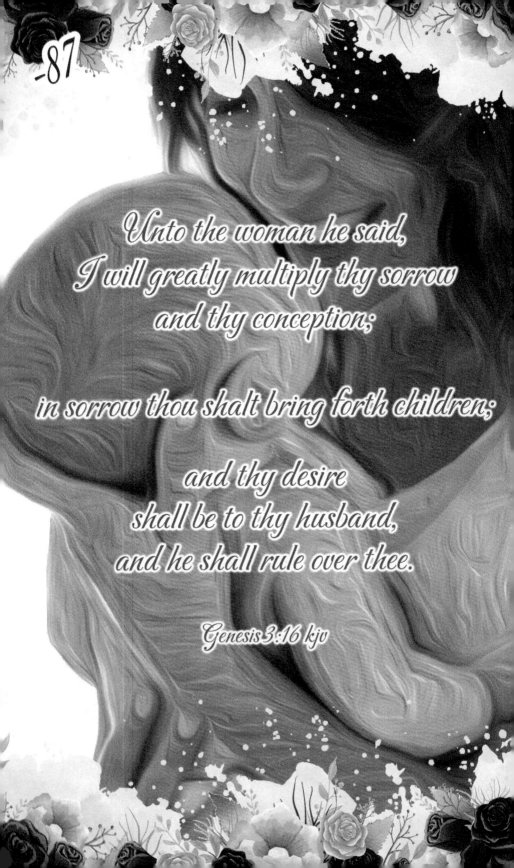

Unto the woman he said,
I will greatly multiply thy sorrow
and thy conception;

in sorrow thou shalt bring forth children;

and thy desire
shall be to thy husband,
and he shall rule over thee.

Genesis 3:16 kjv

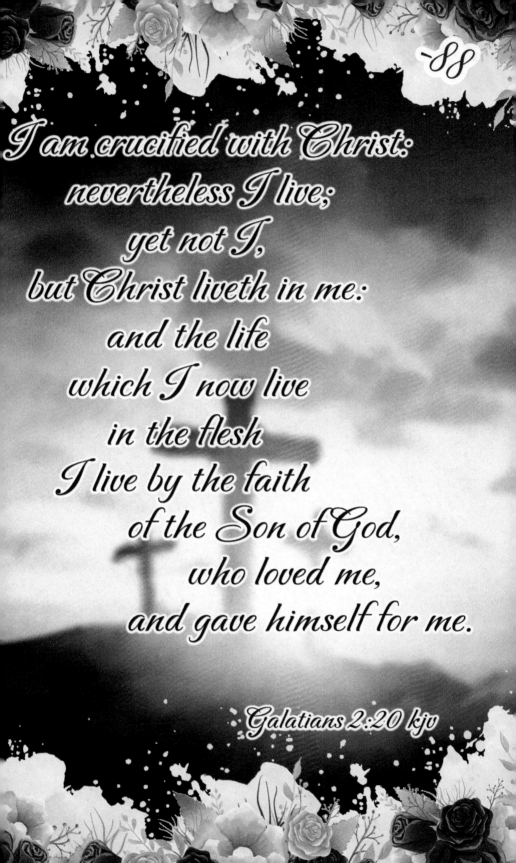

-88

I am crucified with Christ:
nevertheless I live;
yet not I,
but Christ liveth in me:
and the life
which I now live
in the flesh
I live by the faith
of the Son of God,
who loved me,
and gave himself for me.

Galatians 2:20 kjv

Lo,

children are an heritage

of the Lord:

and the fruit of the womb

is his reward.

Psalm 127:3 kjv

Cause me to hear
thy lovingkindness
in the morning;

for in thee do I trust:

cause me to know the way
wherein I should walk;
for I lift up my soul
unto thee.

Psalm 143:8 kjv

And will be
a Father unto you,
and ye shall be
my sons and daughters,
saith the Lord
Almighty.

2 Corinthians 6:18 kjv

Peace I leave with you,

my peace I give unto you:

not as the world giveth,

give I unto you.

Let not your heart be troubled,

neither let it be afraid.

John 14:27 kjv

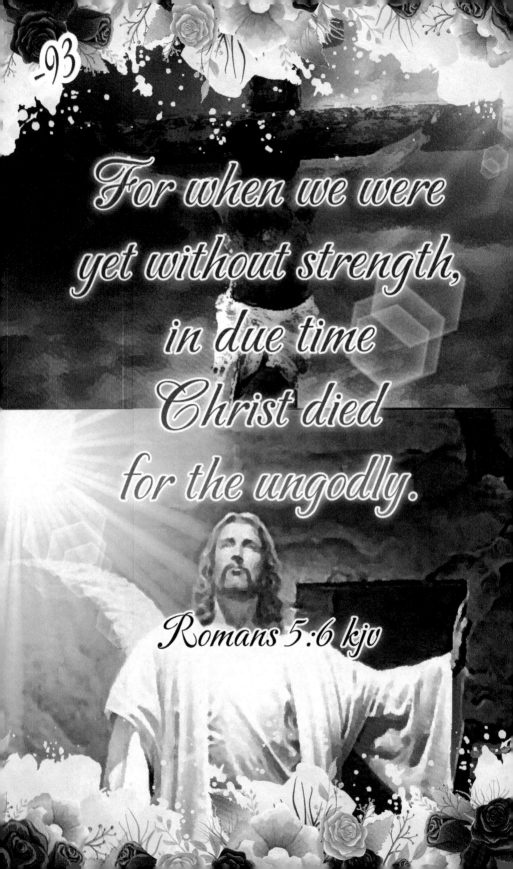

For when we were yet without strength, in due time Christ died for the ungodly.

Romans 5:6 kjv

Favour is deceitful,

and beauty is vain:

but a woman that feareth the Lord,

she shall be praised.

Give her of the fruit

of her hands;

and let her own works

praise her in the gates.

Proverbs 31:30–31 kjv

There is neither Jew nor Greek,

there is neither bond nor free,

there is neither male nor female,

for ye are all one

in Christ Jesus.

Galatians 3:28 kjv

-96

Proverbs 18:22 kjv

Whoso findeth a wife

findeth a good thing,

and obtaineth favour

of the Lord.

To whom God

would make known

what is the riches

of the glory

of this mystery

among the Gentiles;

which is Christ in you,

the hope of glory.

Colossians 1:27 kjv

-98

And if it seem evil unto you
to serve the Lord,
choose you this day
whom ye will serve;

whether the gods
which your fathers served
that were on the other side
of the flood,
or the gods of the Amorites,
in whose land ye dwell:

but as for me and my house,
we will serve the Lord.

Joshua 24:15 kjv

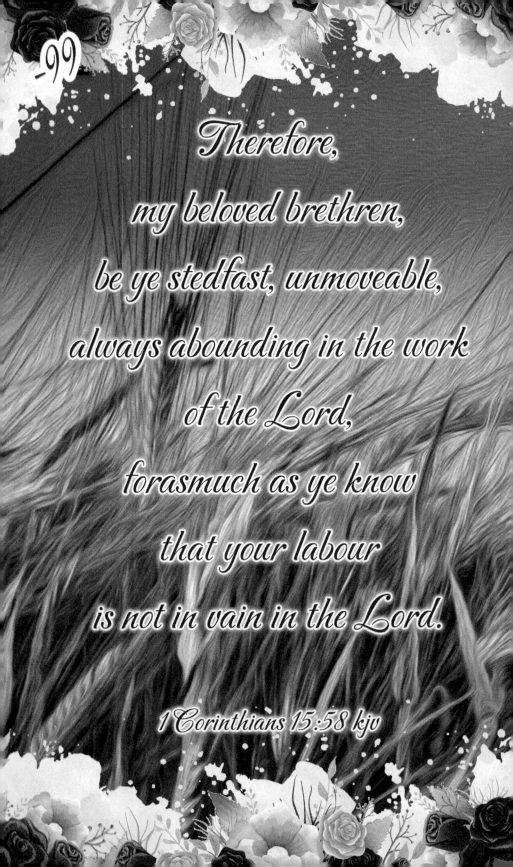

Therefore,
my beloved brethren,
be ye stedfast, unmoveable,
always abounding in the work
of the Lord,
forasmuch as ye know
that your labour
is not in vain in the Lord.

1 Corinthians 15:58 kjv

Charity never faileth:

but whether there be prophecies,

they shall fail;

whether there be tongues,

they shall cease;

whether there be knowledge,

it shall vanish away.

1 Corinthians 13:8 kjv

There shall not any man
be able to stand before thee
all the days of thy life:

as I was with Moses,
so I will be with thee:

I will not fail thee,
nor forsake thee.

Joshua 1:5 kjv

For ye are all the children of God
by faith in Christ Jesus.
For as many of you
as have been baptized into Christ
have put on Christ.

There is neither Jew nor Greek,
there is neither bond nor free,
there is neither male nor female:
for ye are all one in Christ Jesus.

And if ye be Christ's,
then are ye Abraham's seed,
and heirs according to the promise.

Galatians 3:26-29 kjv

103

So God

created man

in his own image,

in the image of God

created he him;

male and female

created he them.

Genesis 1:27 kjv

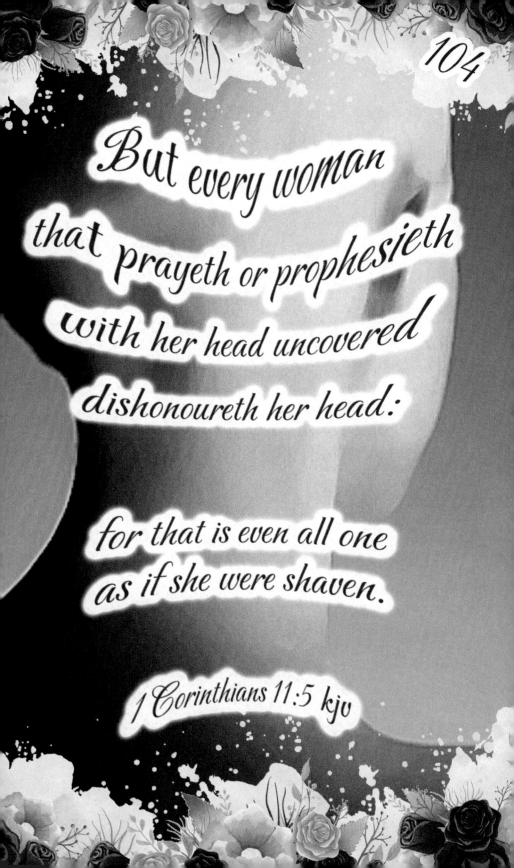

But every woman that prayeth or prophesieth with her head uncovered dishonoureth her head:

for that is even all one as if she were shaven.

1 Corinthians 11:5 kjv

Ephesians 5:22-33 kjv

Wives, submit yourselves
unto your own husbands,
as unto the Lord.

For the husband is the head of the wife,
even as Christ is the head of the church:
and he is the saviour of the body.

Therefore as the church is
subject unto Christ,
so let the wives be to their own husbands
in every thing.

Husbands, love your wives,
even as Christ also loved the church,
and gave himself for it;

That he might sanctify
and cleanse it with the washing of water
by the word,

That he might present it to himself
a glorious church,
not having spot, or wrinkle,
or any such thing;

but that it should be holy
and without blemish.

So ought men to love their wives
as their own bodies.

He that loveth his wife loveth himself.

For no man ever yet hated his own flesh;
but nourisheth and cherisheth it,
even as the Lord...

She is more precious than rubies:
and all the things thou canst desire
are not to be compared unto her.

Length of days is in her right hand;
and in her left hand riches and honour.

Her ways are ways of pleasantness,
and all her paths are peace.

She is a tree of life to them
that lay hold upon her:
and happy is every one
that retaineth her.

Proverbs 3:15–18 kjv

And he began to speak boldly
in the synagogue:
whom when Aquila and Priscilla
had heard, they took him unto them,
and expounded unto him the way
of God more perfectly.

Acts 18:26 kjv

Nevertheless neither is the man without the woman, neither the woman without the man, in the Lord.

For as the woman is of the man, even so is the man also by the woman; but all things of God.

1 Corinthians 11:11–12 kjv

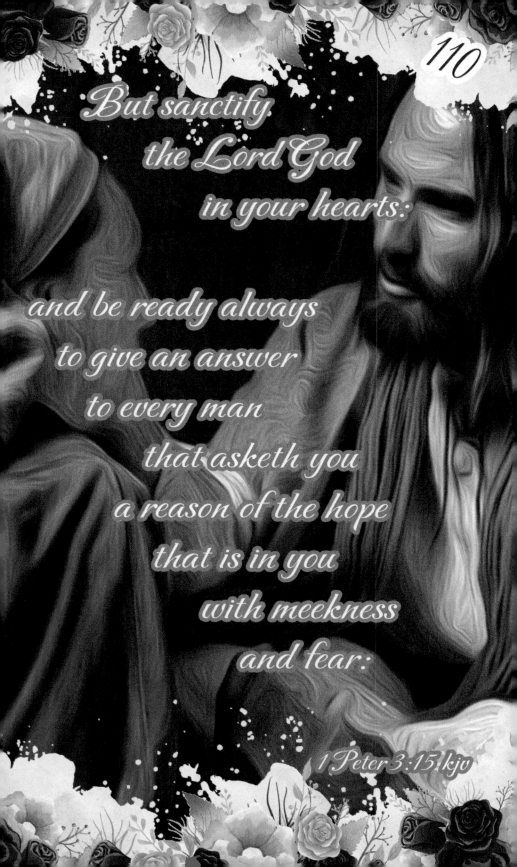

But sanctify
the Lord God
in your hearts:

and be ready always
to give an answer
to every man
that asketh you
a reason of the hope
that is in you
with meekness
and fear:

1 Peter 3:15 kjv

*Likewise,
ye husbands,
dwell with them
according to knowledge,
giving honour unto the wife,
as unto the weaker vessel,
and as being
heirs together of the grace
of life;*

*that your prayers
be not hindered.*

1 Peter 3:7 kjv

Seek the Lord
and his strength,
seek his face
continually.

1 Chronicles 16:11 kjv

Luke 8:1-3 KJV

And it came to pass afterward,

that he went throughout

every city and village, preaching

and shewing the glad tidings

of the kingdom of God:

and the twelve were with him,

And certain women,

which had been healed of evil spirits

and infirmities,

Mary called Magdalene,
out of whom went seven devils,

And Joanna the wife
of Chuza Herod's steward,

and Susanna,
and many others,
which ministered unto him
of their substance.

Therefore shall a man leave his father and his mother; and shall cleave unto his wife: and they shall be one flesh.

Genesis 2:24 kjv

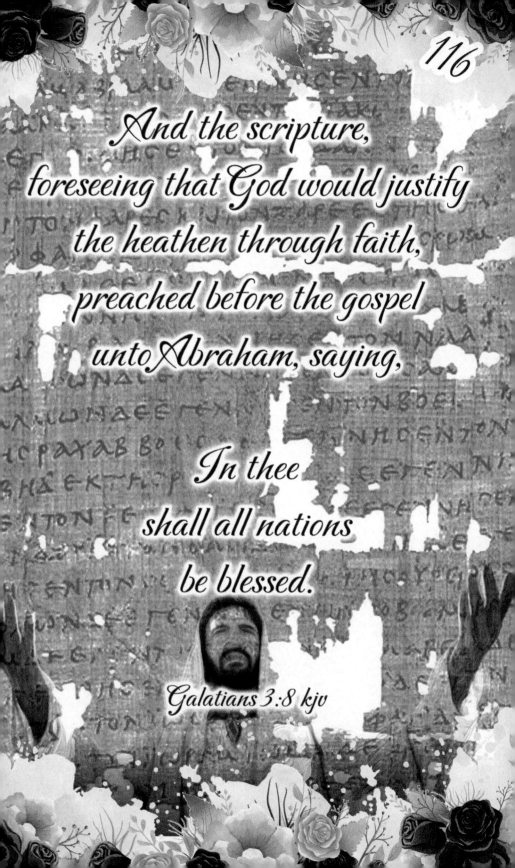

And the scripture,
foreseeing that God would justify
the heathen through faith,
preached before the gospel
unto Abraham, saying,

In thee
shall all nations
be blessed.

Galatians 3:8 kjv

For thou

hast possessed my reins:

thou hast covered me

in my mother's womb.

Psalm 139:13 kjv

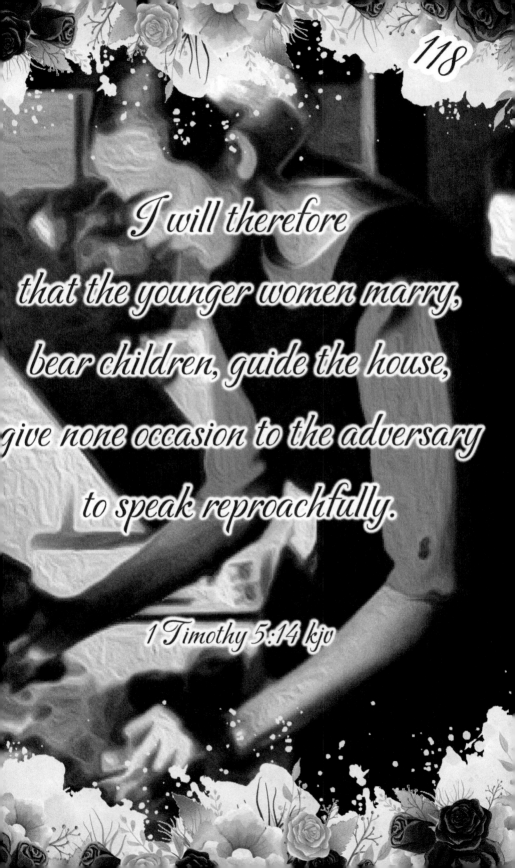

I will therefore

that the younger women marry,

bear children, guide the house,

give none occasion to the adversary

to speak reproachfully.

1 Timothy 5:14 kjv

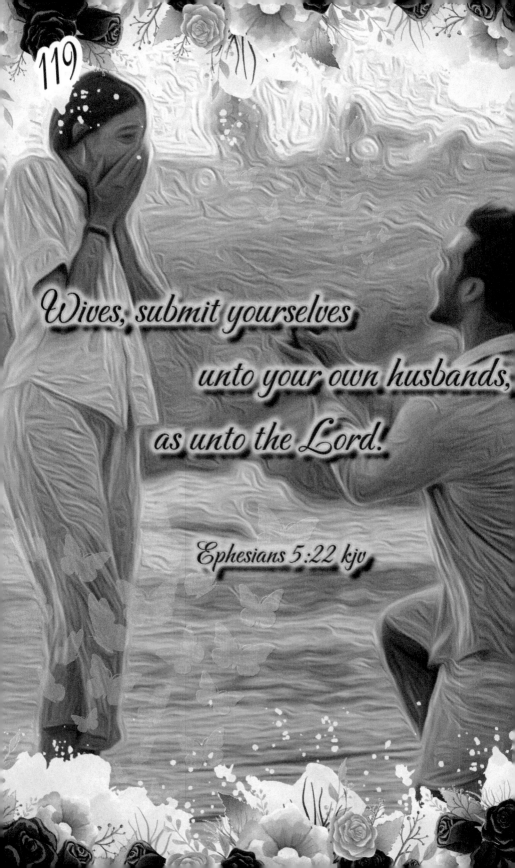

Wives, submit yourselves
unto your own husbands,
as unto the Lord.

Ephesians 5:22 kjv

My son,
keep thy father's commandment,
and forsake not
the law of thy mother:

Proverbs 6:20 kjv

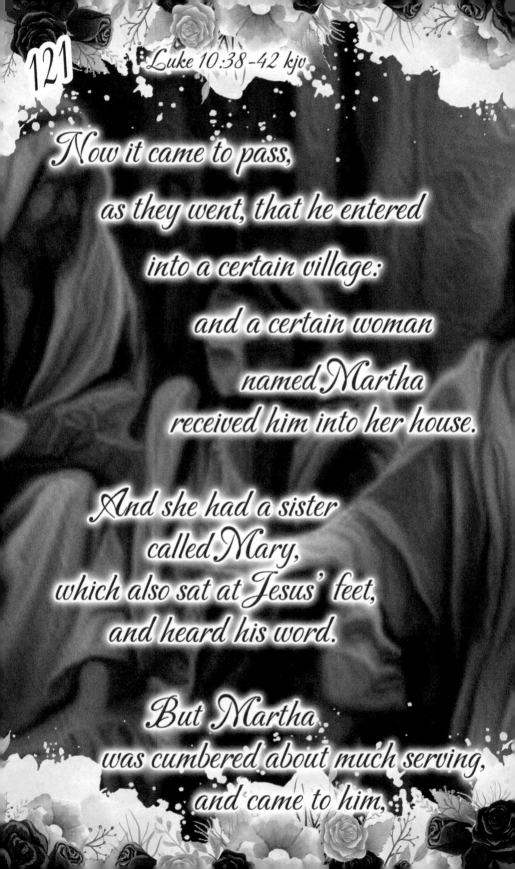

*Now it came to pass,
as they went, that he entered
into a certain village:
and a certain woman
named Martha
received him into her house.*

*And she had a sister
called Mary,
which also sat at Jesus' feet,
and heard his word.*

*But Martha
was cumbered about much serving,
and came to him,*

and said, Lord,
dost thou not care
that my sister hath left me
to serve alone?
bid her therefore
that she help me.

And Jesus answered
and said unto her,
Martha, Martha,
thou art careful and troubled
about many things:

But one thing is needful:
and Mary hath chosen
that good part,
which shall not be taken
away from her.

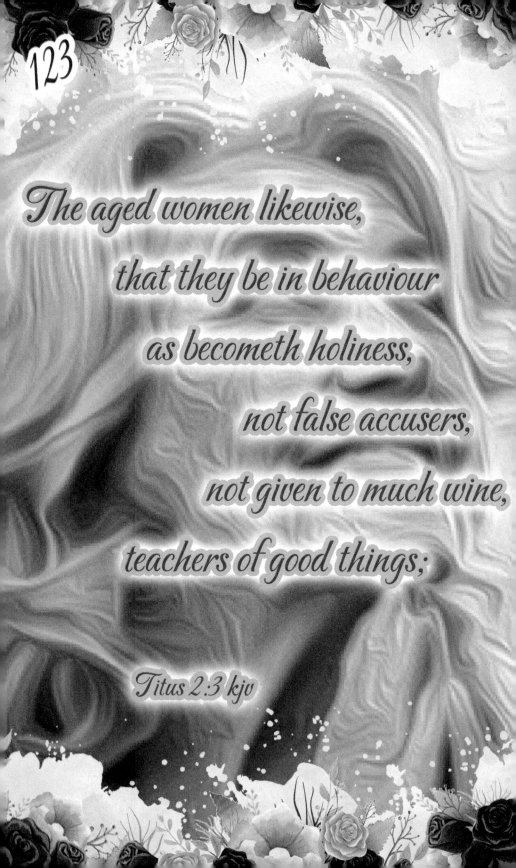

The aged women likewise,

that they be in behaviour

as becometh holiness,

not false accusers,

not given to much wine,

teachers of good things;

Titus 2:3 kjv

As a jewel of gold

in a swine's snout,

so is a fair woman

which is without discretion.

Proverbs 11:22 kjv

Give not thy strength
unto women,
nor thy ways to that
which destroyeth kings.

Proverbs 31:3 kjv

Rebuke not an elder,
but intreat him as a father;
and the younger men as brethren;
The elder women as mothers;
the younger as sisters,
with all purity.

1 Timothy 5:1-2 kjv

When I call to remembrance
the unfeigned faith that is in thee,
which dwelt first
in thy grandmother Lois,
and thy mother Eunice;
and I am persuaded that
in thee also.

2 Timothy 1:5 kjv

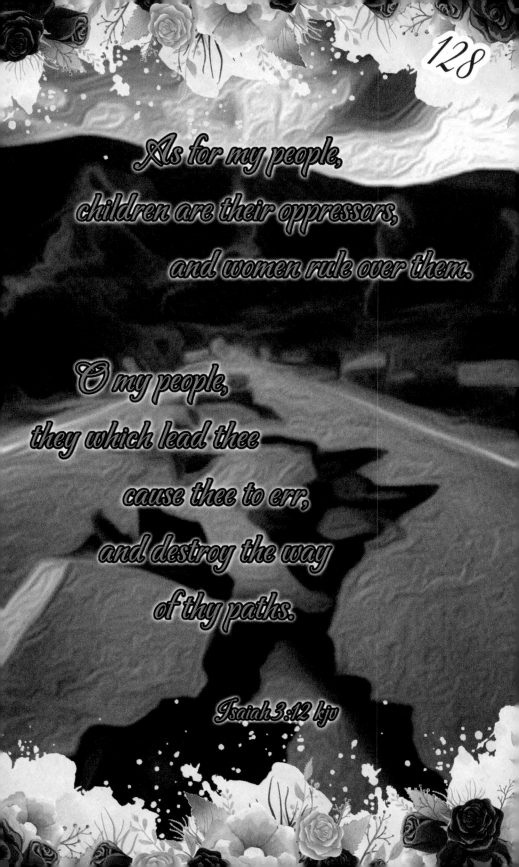

As for my people,

children are their oppressors,

and women rule over them.

O my people,

they which lead thee

cause thee to err,

and destroy the way

of thy paths.

Isaiah 3:12 kjv

And many women
were there beholding afar off,
which followed Jesus from Galilee,
ministering unto him:

Among which was Mary Magdalene,
and Mary the mother
of James and Joses,
and the mother of Zebedees children.

Matthew 27:55-56 kjv

Behold, thou art fair,
my love; behold, thou art fair;
thou hast doves' eyes
within thy locks:
thy hair is as a flock of goats,
that appear from mount Gilead.

Song of Solomon 4:1 kjv

Acts 18:24-26 kjv

And a certain Jew named Apollos,
born at Alexandria, an eloquent man,
and mighty in the scriptures,
came to Ephesus.

This man was instructed
in the way of the Lord;
and being fervent in the spirit,

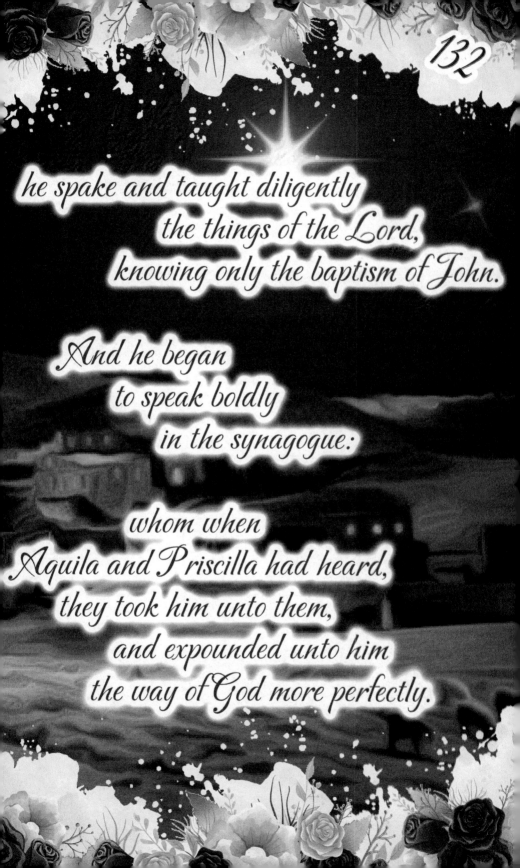

he spake and taught diligently
the things of the Lord,
knowing only the baptism of John.

And he began
to speak boldly
in the synagogue:

whom when
Aquila and Priscilla had heard,
they took him unto them,
and expounded unto him
the way of God more perfectly.

The woman

shall not wear that

which pertaineth unto a man,

neither shall a man

put on a woman's garment:

for all that do so

are abomination

unto the Lord

thy God.

Deuteronomy 22:5 kjv

I commend
unto you Phebe our sister,
which is a servant of the church
which is at Cenchrea:

That ye receive her
in the Lord,
as becometh saints,
and that ye assist her
in whatsoever business
she hath need of you:
for she hath been
a succourer of many,
and of myself also.

Romans 16:1-2 kjv

135

For God so loved the world,

that he gave his only begotten Son,

that whosoever believeth in him

should not perish,
but have everlasting life.

For God sent not his Son
into the world
to condemn the world;
but that the world through him
might be saved.

John 3:16-17 kjv

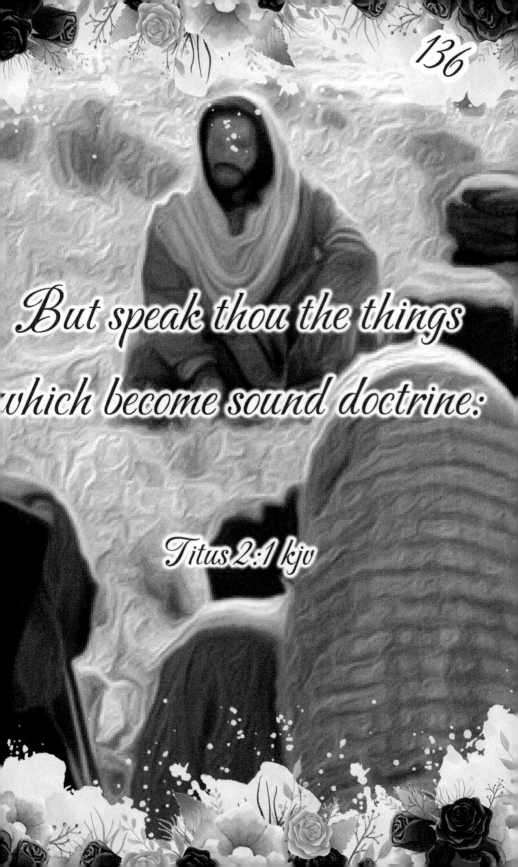

But speak thou the things

which become sound doctrine:

Titus 2:1 kjv

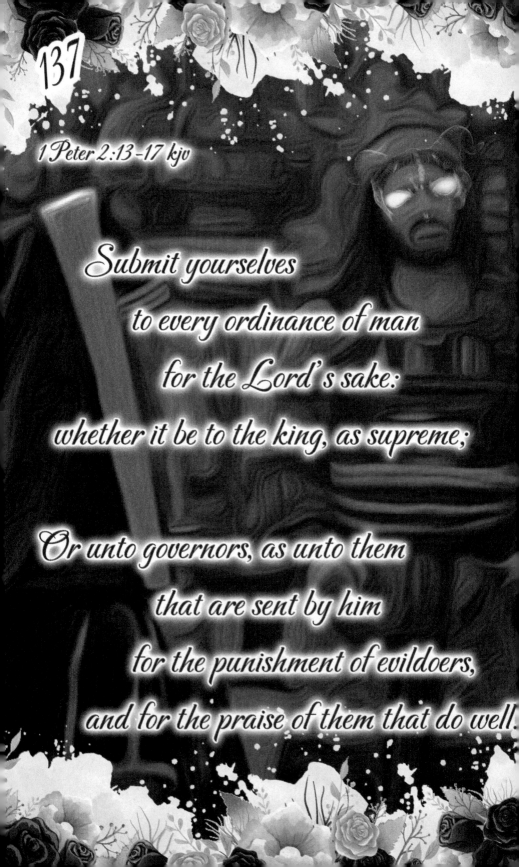

137

1 Peter 2:13-17 kjv

Submit yourselves

to every ordinance of man

for the Lord's sake:

whether it be to the king, as supreme;

Or unto governors, as unto them

that are sent by him

for the punishment of evildoers,

and for the praise of them that do well.

For so is the will of God,
that with well doing
ye may put to silence
the ignorance of foolish men:

As free, and not using your liberty
for a cloke of maliciousness,
but as the servants of God.

Honour all men.

Love the brotherhood.

Fear God.

Honour the king.

139

Acts 1:12–14 kjv

Then returned they unto Jerusalem
from the mount called Olivet,
which is from Jerusalem
a sabbath day's journey.

And when they were come in,
they went up into an upper room,
where abode both Peter,
and James, and John,
and Andrew, Philip,
and Thomas, Bartholomew,

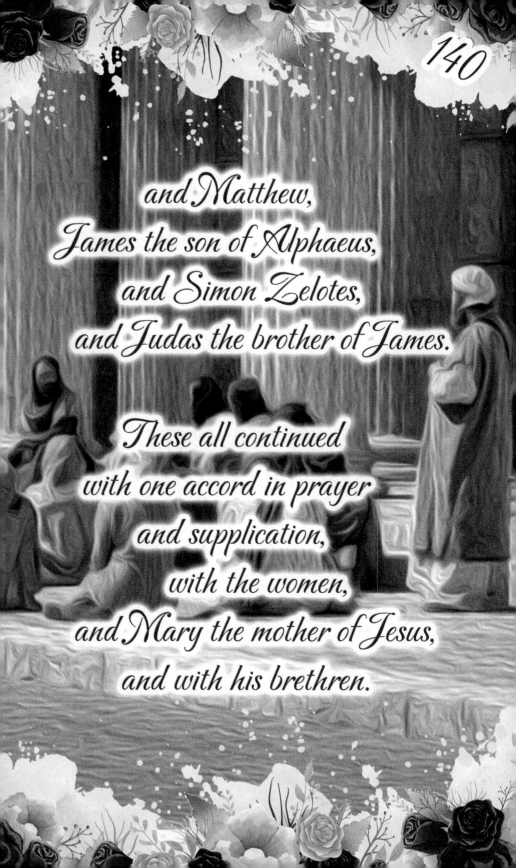

and Matthew,
James the son of Alphaeus,
and Simon Zelotes,
and Judas the brother of James.

These all continued
with one accord in prayer
and supplication,
with the women,
and Mary the mother of Jesus,
and with his brethren.

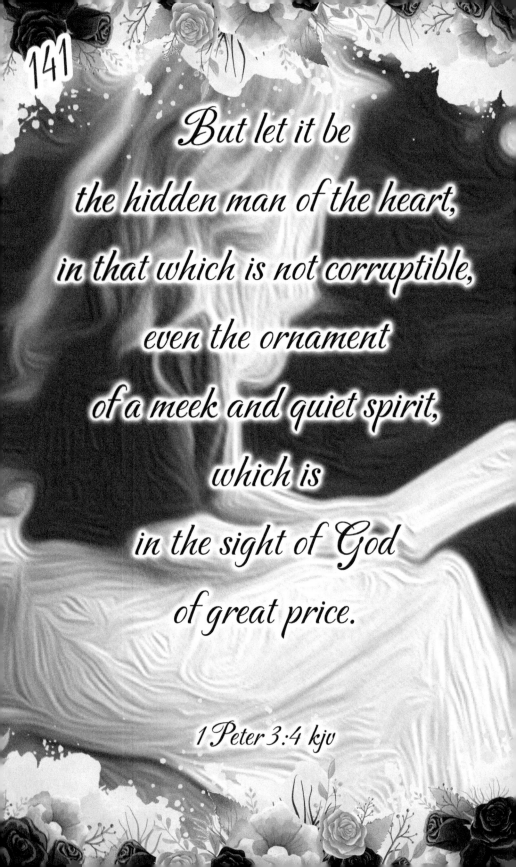

But let it be
the hidden man of the heart,
in that which is not corruptible,
even the ornament
of a meek and quiet spirit,
which is
in the sight of God
of great price.

1 Peter 3:4 kjv

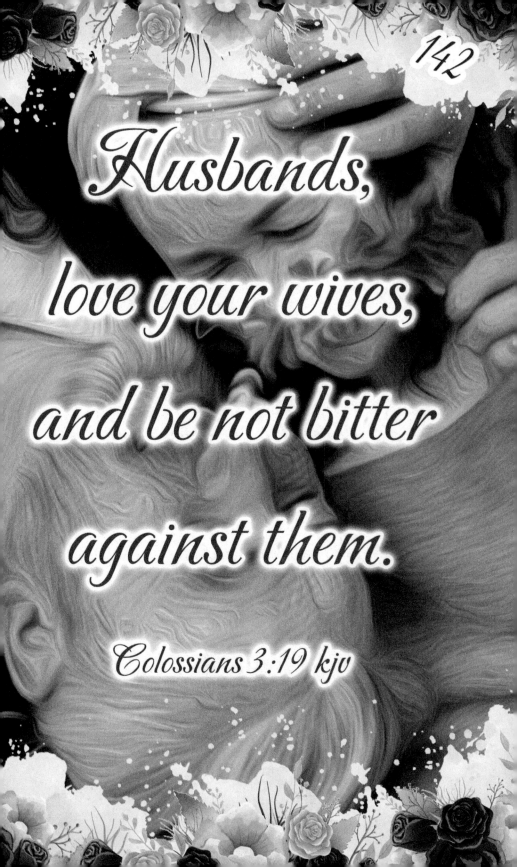

Husbands,

love your wives,

and be not bitter

against them.

Colossians 3:19 kjv

Now therefore
ye are no more
strangers and foreigners,
but fellowcitizens
with the saints,
and of the household
of God;

And are built
upon the foundation
of the apostles
and prophets,

Jesus Christ himself
being the chief corner stone;
In whom all
the building fitly framed together
groweth unto an holy temple
in the Lord:

In whom ye also
are builded together
for an habitation
of God
through the Spirit.

Printed in Great Britain
by Amazon

39424726R00086